CREATING BUSINESS ADVANTAGE

SETTING UP AND RUNNING A SUCCESSFUL BUSINESS

Dear David,
Thanks for all your support and I hope you enjoy!
Daryl

DARYL WOODHOUSE & GARRY SMITH

Creating Business Advantage
Setting Up And Running A Successful Business

ISBN 978-1-909116-43-6

Published in 2015 by SRA Books

A CIP record of this book is available from the British Library.

Printed in the UK by TJ International, Padstow

Contents

A Letter From the Advantage CEO

Dear Reader,

In 2011 after entering the world of extracurricular voluntary mentoring whilst in a full-time employed national leadership position for a FTSE 100 corporation, I identified a real demand for businesses to access diverse but regular expertise and advice to survive and grow into fulfilling their full potential and ambitions. After extensive research, I found that whilst there were some providers for such services available, there was plenty of room for more providers of business coaching, consultancy and training, with advice of the utmost integrity and quality, whilst being affordable to businesses of all shapes and sizes in any sector and at some volume scale. Low and behold, with the help of my wife, best friend and co-director Elizabeth, we formed and registered Advantage Business Partnerships Limited in January 2012 to make a positive difference to the economy with growth advice services to help and support ambitious business owners and their teams to survive, establish and grow.

Garry Smith is one of the founding Business Growth Partners in our experienced, motivated and ambitious team. In our second year of running the business, and following continued research into what businesses need and want from trusted sources of advice, Garry and I found that there was room for a business advice book which spoke more about the day-to-day practicalities of running and growing a successful, profitable business from a simple, guiding perspective. No big rah-rah 'let's conquer the world in three years' approach using 'guaranteed results formulas' and detailed corporate delivery plans.

This is a business book, which goes back to basics on the core and simple principles proven to be required for successful companies.

With our collective business experiences, Garry and I believe that this book will benefit you whether you are the owner of a multimillion business with hundreds of employees, an individual with decision-making responsibilities in a company, or maybe someone about to or thinking about starting up their very first business. Whichever category you fall into, you and your colleagues will find up-to-date, practical knowledge and useful reminders of the simple business functions, which many business leaders and their employees overlook in the race to smash targets and make more money. This book is intended as a prompt to putting your growth ambitions into a holistic commercial business plan including the right basic foundations for building a robust platform to develop your strategy and tactics. Making this work better for you will really help achieve your desired long-term, consistent, sustainable growth. It will also increase your chances of success, and raise the heights of your full potential.

Yours sincerely,

Daryl Woodhouse

Founder and Executive Chairman

Advantage Business Partnerships Limited

Foreword

Holistic Approach to Running a Small Business

For those who have worked in a large company, or a corporate environment, the existence of a myriad of different departments, each one dealing with its own area of the business is not unusual. The way these departments work together in order to deliver for the company is often determined by processes and policies, which ensure integration throughout the organisation.

This luxury is very rarely available to small businesses, with many areas of the business: sales, business development and marketing for example, often seen as departments in their own right, with the approach determined by the dictionary definition of the activity in question.

In this preface we will look at why a holistic approach to sales, business development and marketing is so important to the sustainable success of your business.

> Sales

According to Oxford Dictionaries[1], sales, or more specifically a sale, can be defined as follows:

> ***Sale:*** *Noun – The exchange of a commodity for money.*

1 'Sale.' *Oxford Dictionaries*, 2015. Oxford University Press. Online at: http://oxforddictionaries.com/definition/english/sale?q=sale

A sale, at its core, is indeed the exchange of a commodity, that being in this context a product or service, for payment, but within a business environment it has to be much more than that.

Relationships are absolutely critical to the success of most, if not all businesses in the extremely competitive environment that we currently operate in, and the ability to build mutually beneficial, genuine relationships between your company and your customers should be high on your priority list when recruiting your business development team. Remember, it is these individuals who are likely to be the face of your company out in the marketplace.

By looking at sales from a different angle, to that which is outlined somewhat crudely in the dictionary definition, by integrating your business development strategy effectively and by focussing on the building of the relationship between your company and the customer as your primary objective, the approach to selling becomes much more holistic. It also becomes more of a nice, gentle soft sell, or rather influencing technique, as opposed to the dreaded, brash, confident and 'hard sell' approach.

It is important that the approach you take to selling your product or service is in line with the vision and values of your business, and whilst this will differ for each business, considering sales, business development and marketing as one holistic strategy is an effective way to deliver long-term, sustainable results.

> Business Development

Historically the term business development typically described a number of activities aimed at developing and securing growth opportunities.

In the modern world however, with the ever-increasing volume of customer engagement channels, business development as an activity has had to evolve considerably. It is no longer enough to have business development executives cold-calling prospects from a phone book, or sending out direct mail letters in the local area.

Customers are demanding more from the businesses they buy from, in both the B2B and B2C marketplace, and with competition in many sectors growing by the day alongside record numbers of new start-up businesses, ensuring that your business development strategy is fully integrated with other parts of your business is absolutely critical for success.

Building a relationship between your company and your customer is now considerably more important than simply selling to them, and it's important that your business development strategy focuses on a number of different customer engagement channels in order to build up this connection.

Take Twitter for example. With over 115 million active users per month[2] the potential to engage prospects in a targeted way is very real, but this genuine engagement opportunity is often sacrificed for the desire to sell instantly through what can only be described as spam tweets, with no consideration given to who the end recipient is.

Twitter, of course, is not the only social media channel available, and those who do this correctly across the spectrum will be in the minority. Actively engaging other social media users, whilst not necessarily effective as a direct sales tool, creates a connection between your (prospect) customer and your company, displays the personality behind your business, and contributes to the building of a long-term

2 Twitter Statistics, 2014. *Statistic Brain*. Online at: http://www.statisticbrain.com/twitter-statistics/

relationship; potentially leading to a much higher long-term customer value than would have been achieved from a 'quick sale' approach.

> Always be...

There is a scene in the film *Glengarry Glen Ross (1992)* where Alec Baldwin's character Blake presents his view on what constitutes an effective sales approach:

> A-B-C. A-always. B-be. C-closing. Always be closing. Always be closing.[3]

This hard sell approach has been in existence for a considerable period of time, and still exists in many industry sectors where pressure is high and job security low, but to really deliver long-term, sustainable results for your business, a different approach should be considered. One which takes into account the plethora of different customer engagement channels available; channels where an 'Always be closing' approach would have little to no success as outlined in the Twitter example above.

When setting out your business development strategy, it has to be tightly intertwined with the values of your business, and your business development activities have to reflect this at every opportunity, from the content you post online, to the way your employees conduct themselves both internally and externally.

Almost every interaction with a customer, whether online, face-to-face, over the telephone or through a printed communication is a business development opportunity. Your company values should be at the heart of your business development approach.

Perhaps the acronym should be ABE – Always Be Engaging.

3 *Glengarry Glen Ross*, 1992. Motion picture. New Line Cinema, Los Angeles, CA.

We have now explored why sales is much more than a simple cash for commodities transaction, and how a business development strategy should be expanded into more of a customer engagement strategy in order to extract the most value from business development activities.

We are now going to look at marketing in more detail; what does it actually mean, and how can your marketing strategy be successfully interlinked with both your sales and business development strategy in order to deliver sustainable results for your business.

> Marketing 101

Peter Drucker, an Austrian-born American management consultant, educator and author, said of marketing, 'The aim of marketing is to know and understand the customer so well the product or service fits him and sells itself.'

Customers *want* to engage with the businesses they deal with, and this is why big brands focus so much energy on building emotional connections with customers through social media, or, as Coca-Cola have done only recently, through the actual product itself.

Engaging with your customers and prospects regularly through business development activities, networking or social media for example, is absolutely imperative for those businesses looking to generate high value, sustainable results, but also provides a fantastic opportunity to learn about your customers; how they feel about your product or service, how it helped them, how it could be better.

Understanding the customer so well that the product or service sells itself is certainly the utopian ideal, but using business development activities to genuinely build a two-way relationship with your customers and prospects allows your business to build a much more effective marketing strategy; you won't just 'think' you know what your customers want, you will actually *know*.

Building a marketing strategy without first seeking to understand how best to engage your customers and prospects would be foolish, and this is why integrating your business development activities, where you and your team will learn most about those you are seeking to target, is an important part of the puzzle (strategic market research).

It is this more holistic approach, where business development becomes customer engagement, to generate the inputs to ensure the marketing strategy is effective, which ultimately leads to the 'cash for commodity' sale to help to deliver long-term, sustainable results for your business, in a way that keeping each activity separate does not.

Introduction

There is something very striking in today's economic climate in respect of the upsurge in small business start-ups and a corresponding failure rate. Fifty per cent (yes, 50%) of all business start-ups fail within their first year. After five years the attrition rate is a staggering ninety per cent (yes, 90%). What these figures do not include are the 'zombie' companies – those that continue to survive only because of unprecedented low interest rates and other under the radar factors. This raises the two obvious questions:

1. Why are there so many failures?
2. Can the attrition rate be stemmed?

In the experience of the authors, the answer to the first question has many contributing factors – all of which can be addressed. The answer to the second question is, yes.

Many business failures are due to a lack of experience, or skill, in a number of business areas. The adage of, 'Fail to plan, plan to fail' often applies. Not because there was a deliberate non-action but because it all became overwhelming, and/or the business owner did not know all of the available options.

There are also cases of deliberate, albeit naïve, action causing these failures, whereby the business directors have been determined to minimise costs rather than make calculated and well-researched investment into key suppliers, staff and materials required to maximise the growth opportunities in the local and/or global markets. For example, rather than set up a business Facebook and Twitter account and doing a couple of random tweets to raise awareness of your products, you invest in either outsourcing social media to a proven expert provider, or invest in training for you or a member of your team to learn how to set up and implement a successful social media strategy that really engages with the right prospective customers and engages with them professionally to funnel them to becoming, long-term, loyal customers.

In a large organisation there are specialists concentrating on all of their specific areas of business: finance, HR, product planning, R&D, sales and marketing, production. In a smaller business, all of these required skills often rest with just one or two people.

This book is written as a guide to the issues to be encountered in setting up a new business, or even improving one already large and long established. It is not, however, a manual. There is much detail to understand and apply in the right circumstances and in the right way. As a guide, this book will navigate you to key areas needing more consideration, and will move your planning process towards the right rather than just the correct actions.

The book is divided into chapters, which can be taken as discrete subjects. They do not have to be read in the order in which they appear. It is a 'dipping' book – to be read as the situation dictates. The proof of the pudding will not be a front to back reading but the real test will be how the book helps to formulate ideas and actions to reduce membership of the 50% or 90% group, or better yet for the ambition of Advantage Business Partnerships to turn the five-year failure percentage into a success rate.

This is not a theory book, nor an academic hypothesis. It is written from a position of practical experience gained from working with small/medium and large-sized businesses and helping them to perform to their full potential from board level to junior employee. They say that experience is what you get a split second after you really need it. Well, this book hopes to bring you some of that experience a second *before* you need it. They used to say that learning from your mistakes is the best way to learn. We believe it is better to invest in upskilling yourself through a variety of means such as self-development, reading, or hiring a professional business coach, to then learn from the mistakes of others to stop you making them yourself!

Chapter 1

So, You Have an Idea for a Business

We have all done it at times, either sitting around a dinner table with friends or down the pub; having a conversation and somebody comes up with a great idea for a business. How many of these ideas get any further than the dining table, and if they are such great ideas why haven't they been brought out of conceptualisation? I think we all know the answer – too much hard work, too much risk, too much commitment.

On the other hand, there are people that do pursue their idea for a business out of conceptualisation through to conclusion. What is the difference? The difference is commitment and, to use an overused word, passion. Or, in some cases desperation – this is not a good place to start from unless it is combined with the previous two.

Even having these attributes is not enough. It might be a great idea but is there a commercial market for the product or service and do you have the knowledge, experience and muscle (both influence and financial) to get it to market? We have seen some wonderful pieces of ingenuity and engineering, which solve a problem nobody else seems to have, or certainly not at the selling price required. In other instances we have seen some good ideas flounder with one start-up only to become a major success through a bigger operator. As just one example, a Malaysian electronics company developing reversing sensors for cars and marketing the product as an accessory. This failed to catch on, but when a different company took the same idea and sold it to the car manufacturers, well…

In the current economic climate it is evident that the lack of employment opportunities is making working in one's own business a way of staying in work, or even getting into work. The rules are no different – the world does not make a company successful just because it is a good cause and nobody has yet written a law which makes business survival an absolute guarantee. Every business has to have a product, which it can sell at a profit and in sufficient numbers and frequency to provide a sustainable income. That is true whether you need to earn £500 per week or the income generated is needed to fund exponential growth so that this time next year, like Del and Rodney, you can say 'we are millionaires'.

There is no limit to what ideas can become successful businesses. Once you have identified the need for the product/service, the price/volume/frequency needed and the route to market, and you are confident that you have the commitment, the stamina, the resources, the commercial knowledge and the support (family, friends and the right business team) to see the idea through, then proceed beyond Go. But be careful not to end up in Jail or out of the game. You might be lucky and draw a few favourable Community Chest cards on the way but it is how you play what is in front of you that will really count.

Chapter 2

How Do You Start a Business?

Without question – seek professional advice. Consider what relevant experience or professional training you have had towards starting, running, growing and profitably exiting businesses. Are you a highly motivated fool? Be honest in identifying your skills and knowledge gaps. Do some reading; get some training. Get advice on the areas you know little about from people who do know. Remember also that 'You don't know what you don't know'. Don't rely too heavily on what you think you should know and do. Move yourself to a position of knowing what you need to know and do.

Even if your business idea is going to see you working from your kitchen table as a sole trader, still go and get some advice from at least a successful business coach, a knowledgeable accountant and probably a trustworthy lawyer as well. The decisions you make at this stage are the foundations for what you build going forward. It is that important.

At the simplest level a sole trader status can be set up quickly and without too much formality. But how do you know that it is the correct format for what you want to achieve? There are tax implications, implications on your ability to borrow funds for the business, and implications on you as an individual being inseparable from the business. Just one for instance: How much tax relief can you claim for using part of your home as an office?

If you are not a sole trader but perhaps you have gone into a partnership with your best friend, then how do you structure the arrangement correctly? Are you equal partners and to what extent?

Do you have an agreement on what will happen given possible, and definite, circumstances into the future (e.g. dispute, critical illness)? These are all things that need to be considered *now* while you are friends, still alive and in a position to discuss issues without emotion. There are too many enemies out there who used to be the best of friends. Business gets tough, personal relationships start to get in the way, you want to take different paths and then find that the decisions you took in the beginning don't give you a fair share, or influence, on the way forward from where you find yourself. It could have all been so different. Maybe the correct legal entity for you is a limited liability partnership. Maybe it is a limited company. Maybe it is a charity, or a social enterprise.

I am not dismissing the operational aspects of getting a business started. Of course you will have to launch the business in an appropriate way to announce the arrival of your product/service offered to your prospective customers. The website will have been designed, your advertising planned, your networking commenced, your business plan written, and all the myriad of activities that will become your daily focus of attention in the time ahead scheduled into your diary. Of course it is crucial to get these things underway as, without them, your business will still be an idea. However, if you don't get these things right the first time, there will be opportunities to make changes. It would be better if you got it right the first time and then worked on continuously improving to avoid regretting a past inaction that cannot be made better without significant revenue and time loss. The message here is to take time to fully understand your business and its direction and then set it up accordingly as best as you can. Do not legally form your business and then plan its operation.

The importance of how you start your business cannot be over-emphasised. Your understanding of what your business does and what you need to do to get customers is the easy, visible, obvious, transparent and challenging aspect. It is what you set out to do in forming the business. However, designing the house of your dreams and then building foundations on sand will soon have cracks through every wall. To the contrary, it is argued that nothing and no one is perfect so do not plan for ultimate perfection. Plan for near perfection. The time you take to get your product or service from 85% perfect to 100% perfect could be the timeframe someone else uses to take a similar concept to market at 80% perfection. It is a careful balance.

Chapter 3

Know Your Destination

Using the idea of plotting a destination on a map is an old analogy used in business planning, but that is not to say it doesn't serve well. Like Columbus, who knew where he was leaving from and had a good idea of where he was heading, we sometimes find something along the route, which is far more interesting and profitable than the original destination. However, if we don't know where we are starting from, and set out prepared to only follow our noses then how can we ever hope to arrive at the place we were aiming for and recognise greater opportunities that present themselves along the way?

In business the point about knowing where you are starting from is vitally important. You have to know the state of the market and your place in it to enable your business proposition to get away from the starting line. Research the size of your potential market and its expected future performance. Understand the demographics of your target clients including age, geography, affordability, personalities and also, how do your clients want to be approached? It is no use entering a mature market with an unremarkable product and truckloads of ambitious 'hope' to make in-roads. That is tantamount to saying 'If I was going there I wouldn't start from here.' You are where you are and you have to work with that. Look at how you make your product different, your customer service remarkable and your reliability exceptional.

As part of knowing your market, you must know how good (or bad) your competitors are, to focus on how your products and services can be far greater. However, do not rely purely on quality as something that will differentiate you from your competition. In today's world, achieving good quality in the majority of areas of your business will only get you onto the playing field – it will not get you star billing.

Having established where you are, you can now decide upon your destination. Do not set your destination in strictly business terms. In all likelihood you will outlive your business, so does it have to provide you with a pension? It may be that your destination is to build the business over a short timescale, let's say five years, and then sell it for an enormous profit to a big multi-national. If so, then your plan needs to include a detailed picture of what the business has to achieve in that time to be attractive to such a buyer at your desired price.

Here is something we have touched upon in chapter 2: if you are in a partnership, do all of the partners have the same ambition? Does your shareholder agreement allow for a situation where one of the partners wishes to leave at a point in time while the other partner(s) continue? It is not uncommon for a set of owner/directors to have not discussed with each other how they wish to exit the business. If one wants to retire at, let us say 60, while the other(s) wants the business to be continued by their children, then is this really a possibility given the way the company is structured?

Be very clear on your destination. You may not get there, but if you know where you want to go, you can make the informed decision of how far away from the route you are and what you need to do to get back on track, or you may decide that where you have ended up is a better place and serves you more advantageously. But, unlike Columbus, if you do end up somewhere different from your intended destination don't think that you have arrived where you set out to be (there is a big difference between India and America).

Chapter 4

How Do You Get the Right Funding?

How many people know the significance of the small medium enterprise (SMEs) in the British economy? The sector accounts for 58.8% of private sector employment, 99% of all companies, and contributes £1.5 billion towards GDP. The importance of SMEs cannot be overstated. Despite the large contributions of UK small and medium enterprise, there is the persistent barrage of claims from the government, on the one hand, about measures to help small businesses, and on the other hand the claims from small business owners that they cannot access the finance or tax breaks they need to grow and establish themselves.

Let us be clear: funding is available but not necessarily from the traditional lenders, i.e. the big banks. If you have a business that has been trading for at least two years and you have maintained a good credit rating for the business then there are numerous options out there to suit different circumstances.

The issue is somewhat different if you are a start-up business with no track record. Banks will not lend to the business until you have at least six months of history with them, and many finance houses will look for the two years' experience. So where do you go with your business idea to get the necessary funding to get started? And also how do you avoid a 'dragon's den' offer of two balloons and a goldfish for 90% of the business.

The first thing you have to determine is, are you ready for funding? Now this will sound like an insult when you have thought long and hard about the business, where you want it to go, what you want it to be, and what it will return as shareholder value. You have written your business plan and completed a cash flow forecast for the first three years together with a profit and loss forecast. But are you ready for funding?

Keep one very important thing in mind when considering what to do. You are now a business owner – how much emotion and sympathy would it take for you to risk your money on a promise? On the other hand, if you are presented with a plan that answers a need with a product and service, is targeted at the right customer population, is priced correctly (not necessarily the cheapest), has a sustainable gross profit from a proven track record of sales including growth over several years and the owners can demonstrate their confidence in the business by previously putting some of their own skin into it, then you have a business ready for funding.

The last point is important – if you as a business owner are seeking money from others and cannot, or will not, demonstrate your confidence in the business success with your own stake (savings, investment, offering property as security in the event of business failure) then how can the lender or investor have confidence that their money is being put to good use and will be relatively safe as an investment? You have to demonstrate this in your search for funding. This should have gone without saying but it is quite alarming how many new business owners expect not to carry any risk.

The getting ready for finance phase is crucially important and needs to be right in all respects to gain a positive response from potential lenders/investors. Advice is out there to help you through the maze. Making use of that advice will improve your chances of gaining funding for a robust business idea. Slowing down your ambitions for global success and business award recognition in order to take longer to get the right strategy and business model, will not only increase your long-term growth potential and likelihood of survival, it will also give you more influence to negotiate more preferential terms with lenders or investors. Another thing, those stairs out of the dragon's den look awfully steep to me.

Chapter 5

Location, Location, Location

Never mind the TV programme, it was Charles Forte whose maxim was location, location, location as he expanded the Forte Hotel chain. And in his day he was absolutely right. Even today in the virtual world of the Internet it still holds true – in a virtual interpretation.

Not all businesses require the same type of location. Your business will determine your ideal location(s). If we look back to the Industrial Revolution, industries were established close to the energy sources needed to fuel them and the raw materials needed to process into goods. Today that situation has changed somewhat but location remains important for other reasons.

A logistics company will not want to be located in the middle of a city with the inherent traffic congestion to negotiate before getting underway to the destinations. An ice cream stand will want to be on the beachfront and not down a back alley a mile from the sea. An Internet retailer will want to be on page 1 of the search engine rankings and not buried at page 36.

Location remains a hugely important factor in the potential success of your business. As an example, a new grille restaurant and coffee bar was being proposed for a town centre location. The demographics are right for this kind of business, but exact positioning was crucial for the success of the business. Different premises were considered before deciding upon a shop that is in a pedestrian precinct just outside of the main shopping mall. It is a thoroughfare for students moving between university accommodation and university, it has a high footfall of potential customers walking from the car parks and bus stops into the main shopping street and mall, and it is close to the nightlife of the town. Another option was premises close to the railway station. This was decided against because it had low footfall (all transport went past and didn't stop nearby), potential customers were those in a hurry and were more likely to buy coffee at the railway station, and it was secluded from the main activities of the town centre. The two premises are 200 metres apart.

In the virtual world the principle is exactly the same. You have to be accessible to your customers – they have to be able to find you. Choose your .co.uk or .org or .com carefully. If you are targeting export orders then is .co.uk a suitable domain when, in many countries, being identified immediately as British can have the effect of being passed over without even looking at what you have to offer.

Don't take location for granted. It will either make your business or break it. Be specific, as the example above aims to demonstrate. Above all, ensure that your location allows your customers to get to you conveniently and meets all of their needs, and on a continual basis, because so many external factors can cause the best situation today to change tomorrow. Also make sure that you can service your customers unhindered by by-laws, traffic restrictions, planning issues, and the wrong postcode/domain.

Chapter 6

Competitive Advantage

Try thinking about competitive advantage when looking for somewhere to eat in a location you do not know and where you do not speak the language. What is it that attracts you into one restaurant rather than any other that you have walked past? It can't be the message in the signage, because you don't understand it. Maybe it is simply a case of finding somewhere that has a lot of customers who look happy, the place looks clean, and you can see a table available. Whatever it is, that particular restaurant has won your business for that night. If it lives up to its promise it may have won your custom for the remainder of your stay in that town.

We are not suggesting that all competitive advantage is intuitive. There is so much information available to customers today that they find out about you and your competition without moving from their home or office. They can compare your business offering with other companies and can also read what customers thought about each of the companies that they are considering. One effect of this is probably to have people focussing on price. How many times do you hear the comment 'I could have got it cheaper on the internet.' Our view is that it is not just price that determines the winner of the purchase. The website itself will have played a significant part in building the prospective customer's confidence in the business in the way that it presented the information, the site's functionality and the way it made promises about delivery, transparency or some other virtue aimed at enticing the customer into a deal, e.g. online discount codes.

For that reason we think that Michael Porter's model of competitive advantage remains an accurate means by which to determine how you will make your company distinctive and win business away from your competitors. The new dimension is that your competitors are now not just within the close geographical area – they can almost be anywhere in the world. If you are reading this thinking 'I'm not a restaurant owner, so how is this relevant to me?' then stop and think carefully for some moments. Take these examples and tailor them in your own mind according to your business type and your customers'.

With price not being the only factor, what else is there that will have customers coming to you, and coming back to you?

- Is your product different or can it be substituted with another commodity? Does it offer a unique feature, a new experience or a longer life in operation? Think about choosing your next car; they are all only boxes on wheels – aren't they?
- Does it bring value for money to your ideal target audience if not the lowest price?
- Does your product or service portray a brand and attraction in tune with your chosen client type? For example, is it funky, fresh and cool enough to appeal to the kids? Or if you are targeting a high-net-worth businessman, is it perhaps strong, confident, and eloquently bold?
- What about the service you deliver every time to every one of your customers? Can you be relied upon to meet your promises? Think about after-sales experiences too (missed or just below par in many businesses in most sectors – the professional services and banking/finance usually fail at this).
- Are you more efficient and effective than the rest? Can you deliver more quickly, and more reliably?

All in all, your complete offering must offer value for money when all of the constituent parts are considered together. That is how your customers will view it. Just the same as choosing where to eat – only this time they will be in their hometown and know the language, the menu and your reputation through channels such as local knowledge and online ratings.

Chapter 7

Managing Time

In running a business what you have to achieve and the time available in which to do it is like pushing sticky tar uphill. Time is also like water running through your fingertips; what you have had is gone and what is to come is for you to make the most of. If you waste it, you cannot get it back. But you've heard all of this before. We bet you have also said 'There are not enough hours in the day.' Managing our time is critical if we are to do all of the things that we need to do and still get to bed in the same day.

Effective time management requires self-discipline. This not purely a case of getting up early and working late, it is about having a clearly-defined plan with prioritised activities and sticking to it. It also means putting those things that you are dreading doing at the top of your to-do list and doing them in that order. What a working lifetime has taught us is that if you tackle the dreaded tasks first while you are fresh then they are never as bad as you thought and take half the time you thought it would take to resolve. Be brave. Be focused.

This is a general principle for tackling and prioritising all activities. Get the big and least enjoyable ones done first. You will find it the same as putting a hard-core base down for your new driveway. If you put the big bits in first and then the small ones, somehow the small ones find places for themselves and you have a flat bed on which to surface. On the other hand, if you put the small bits in first then the surface looks like a reconstruction of the Himalayas. In addition, whilst you might not like sales calls, there are many people out there that do. If you don't like administration, there are many others that do. Hire someone to do the jobs you dislike and are inefficient at, or outsource it. Think about value in delegating these tasks too. If you can achieve sales of £100.00 in an hour of your time, you can give the accompanied paperwork to a skilled office person at say, £25.00 an hour, leaving you with £75.00 to play around with. You will then have been both time efficient and cost effective within the same action.

'There are always too many interruptions during the day' we hear you say. Well, manage them. There are many techniques for doing this. For example, the manager who had a dagger on his desk. If the dagger lay flat on the desk then he was OK to approach with whatever subject you had. On the other hand, if the dagger was stuck point down into the desk – beware. Work colleagues who did not deploy a 'Do not disturb' technique never understood why he arrived later than anyone else and went home earlier, until later on. Please note, we encourage you not to have weapons in your workplace! Try a toy police siren or something less threatening; on for do not disturb, off for I am available. Other simple examples of minimising distractions include, turning your phone off or putting it on silent in meetings or during laborious priority office-based tasks, and also switching off new email pop ups in your outlook calendar so you can concentrate on one email or task at a time. Book short, focused time slots into your calendar for checking in on emails and returning calls.

The subject of priority is fundamental to managing your time better. Learn to understand the difference between 'urgent' and 'important'. Because something is 'urgent' means that it needs to be dealt with sooner, it does not mean to say that it needs a lot of time spent on it. Something that is 'important' does. Look out carefully for the situation that is both 'urgent' and 'important'.

We are not naturally list people, but agree that there is something quite satisfying in starting the day/week with a list and crossing off all the items that have been achieved. Also by adding additional things that we have done in a different colour ink so that at the end of the day you can highlight if you achieved, underachieved, or even overachieved. Rewarding yourself for overachievements, which might be as simple as an extra tea break or a luxury biscuit, can make a big difference to morale and motivation. Or better still – going home earlier and coming in later like the dagger manager!

Unless you are the only person in your business then you don't have to do everything. Your partners and employees are there to share the workload. Don't be frightened to delegate with responsibility, but never abdicate. Lead and inspire, asking politely for support rather than being the bossy, dictatorial manager. Explain the rationale, importance and level of urgency behind each task to those sharing your workload. That will help them understand your style and think better, whilst developing their commercial understanding of the business. All of this will provide you with even more time and better employee engagement with improved staff retention.

We all know the effects of stress on our decision-making capabilities. Maintain an environment where you remain in control to make the decisions that matter to your business and don't become the March Hare from *Alice in Wonderland* – always late for a very important date.

Chapter 8

Sales or Marketing

There was an argument some years ago as to whether it should be 'Sales and Marketing' or 'Marketing and Sales'. We don't think that this came about because a realisation was dawning that customers were becoming far more discerning and informed in their choices and that to make a sale was no longer a case of presenting oneself in front of a customer and doing a deal, it also underlined the fact that marketing is more than advertising. Nonetheless, surely the marketing of a service must come before a sale is completed, so we would argue it is ordered as 'Marketing and Sales'.

In the foreword we discussed a holistic approach and as a small business that is the way you manage your total business, but be sure that you know when you are marketing and when you are selling. Even if you are a market trader you still are marketing. Think about it – why is it that you can attract buyers to your stall rather than them going to another? Is it your traditional grafter 'gift of the gab' with your chants of 'Come and see what I have for you here' that attracts people along to see what it is, or is it the appearance of your stall and the signage that you have selected to display your wares. Either way, what you have done is to create an engagement with your potential customers and draw them to you for you to be able to conclude a deal and complete a sale, or from their perspective, complete a purchase. However, what you have also been trying to establish during your sales pitch is a relationship with your customer – one that will have them coming back to you time and time again because you have responded to their needs.

In simple terms you cannot have sales without marketing. If your potential customers do not know that you exist then you will not get any footfall to your business. If you don't get enough footfall then you will not sell enough to keep your business alive. This is true whether you have a physical store or an Internet store. There is not one channel for marketing – the trick is to determine the channels that your potential customers utilise. And don't be dismissive of your audience. I saw an advertisement on a tube train some time ago promoting a portal site for people to explore the options available for receiving care. One passenger exclaimed that they are not going to find many customers on a train. Another replied that whilst his mother was in need of care she would not see the advertisement, however, he (the poorly mother's son) was the one who would be making the arrangements and found the advertisement of use. This also makes the point that you need to be sure that you know who your customer really is – it might not be the end user. This will, importantly, affect the message that you communicate.

Probably the most famous model of marketing is that of Kotler, who identified four elements within what he termed 'The Marketing Mix: product, price, promotion and place'[4]. We argue that people are an equally important part of the mix. However, what this demonstrates is that the mix has to be balanced with your overall strategy. It is of no use promoting your product in terms of lowest price available when you have set out to establish high margins across an optimum volume of sales. This also hints at not taking a scattergun approach but rather to be selective on your targets. In that way you can be specific to your potential customers and communicate with them more accurately and appealingly. This will leave the selling to be about the detail.

4 Kotler, P. (1996) *Marketing Management Analysis, Planning, Implementation, and Control (The Prentice Hall International series in marketing)*. Pearson Education.

The last word of warning is this, marketing and sales are not straight-line processes. What is learned about customers in sales, needs to be fed back to marketing to make sure that the channels are being used to the best and most profitable effect and the same must be applied in reverse.

Marketing is about creating a population of interested potential customers. Selling is about converting them and maintaining them as customers.

Chapter 9

What Marketing Really Means

You have done it now. You have started your own business and created your own marketing department. But what does it do for you? If you think it is about advertising then think again. Marketing is all about: analysis, planning, implementation, and control. To do this you also need to understand your marketing mix (Kotler).

Marketing is an integral part of your business – it is not an add-on. Without marketing, in whatever form is appropriate, you will have no customers and no business. Marketing is about communicating with your potential customers and attracting them to buy your output. It is also about gaining preference from your customers over your competition so that they buy from you and not them.

To be successful in marketing and business, you have to align your business throughout so that everything is consistent. It is no good having a high cost base and competing with a low price. Something will have to change.

So what is this marketing mix? Kotler defines four elements to the mix: price, place, promotion, and product. You can also add a fifth dimension: people. Without people and understanding their needs, desires, motivations, how are you going to communicate with them effectively?

Your marketing endeavours must epitomise your strategy. If you have decided that your strategy is (to quote Michael Porter) a price differentiation strategy, then price will be the major element of your marketing mix. If, however, you have decided upon a technology differentiation, service differentiation, or any other form of distinguishing yourself from your competitors then that will decide upon your marketing mix, how you communicate and to whom you communicate. Marketing is a result of strategy and not a strategy in itself. It is, nonetheless, true that analysis of the elements in your marketing mix may lead you to produce something that fits to a different market segment than was originally decided upon and it will certainly influence your service or product development plans. However, whatever your marketing does do it has to be achievable and be consistently delivered, reviewed and adjusted by the total business.

Marketing relies on a clear understanding of your business strategy. It requires that it be communicated accurately, and enticingly, to your customers in order to persuade them that you have what they want/need, and that it meets all of their expectations for reliability, service, accessibility, price and quality. Marketing is derived from your total business strategy and will also influence it tactically. It will provide the analysis of your marketplace, the plans to be relevant to your customers, the implementation of that communication and the control through the business to ensure that all areas are aligned and are delivering the expectations raised with all customers. If it doesn't do that then your business will fail the customers.

Chapter 10

The Importance of People in Every Respect

Unless you are a hermit and your business has no customers, you will have to deal with people. In fact, it is more than that – you will have to be successful with people. This includes all the people that can directly influence your life and business: family, friends, customers, prospects, suppliers, advisors, co-directors, employees and maybe even subcontractors!

There is an old adage that 'people do business with people' and even in today's virtual, cyber, digital world this is still true. You may do all of your business over the Internet but unless you are communicating with your potential customers then they will not stay on your site, if they even get to it in the first place. Facebook, Twitter, LinkedIn – whatever channel you use the clue is in the title of 'social media'. Social, as in people together. Yes, society. You can't get away from it, you can't ignore it and you certainly cannot be successful without being good at it.

If you have employees you have three duties towards them:

- communicate,
- motivate, and
- control.

Your employees are there to do a job for you – for which you pay them a wage. That's the deal. However, your interaction with them will have a direct impact on how they perform the job you need them to do. You will want them to be loyal, diligent, hardworking and productive. This will not just happen by giving them a contract. The way you talk to them, talk to customers, interact with suppliers, listen to advisors and react to situations in the business will either indicate to your team how you want the business to be or it will turn them off and you will not get the outputs that you are paying for. In one paragraph I cannot convey the complex situation of an employer/employee relationship. There are thousands of books out there on the subject, but what you should understand is that your employees' performance is as much to do with you as it is to do with them.

It is similar with suppliers. This time you have to realise that you are the customer and have every right to be treated as you would treat any of your customers. But remember, this is a business-to-business relationship and will be founded on contracts and processes. That said, if you need something a little bit special from your supplier, such as a large order at short notice for a significant new client win or maybe a temporary flex to your credit terms, then it will be your personal relationship that will determine how responsive they are to your need.

We have already mentioned customers, but it is worth saying a little more. You not only need to relate to them through your advertising and promotional material, you also need to relate to their needs throughout the period of the transaction and that includes after-sales service. You keep customers by exceeding their expectations and you lose them not only by direct results but by reputation as well. If you do a good job they will tell two friends, if you do a bad job they will tell eleven friends and socially share it, potentially globally via the Internet.

Don't get us wrong, we are not proposing that all business people should study sociology and psychology or aspire to be a social paragon, but the bare truth is that in business people are crucially important. This is equally true whether the people are customers, suppliers or employees. All have to be managed if your business is to succeed. And people skills are what you need. There is another saying, 'In business you don't get what you deserve, you get what you negotiate.'

Chapter 11

Leadership vs. Management

As a small business owner you will know that you have to wear many hats in running your business. The thing is that leadership and management are not the same hat. You need to be able to wear both, but you also need to know when each of them is most appropriate.

> ***Leadership:*** *Noun – the action of leading a group of people or an organisation, or the ability to do this.*

Whereas,

> ***Management:*** *Noun – the process of dealing with or controlling things or people.*

Interpreted through our own business experiences, we feel an example of an effective leader compared against an average manager may help illustrate a more relevant context than the Oxford definitions[5] above. For us, an effective leader could be someone who inspires and leads people to happily outperform trends and objectives. A successful leader rolls up his or her sleeves showing and teaching his or her team how to do what is required, helping them along the way and encouraging them to innovate by bringing their own personalities, ideas and style. An average performing manager often

5 'Leadership.' *Oxford Dictionaries*, 2015. Oxford University Press. Online at: http://www.oxforddictionaries.com/definition/english/leadership

'Management.' *Oxford Dictionaries*, 2015. Oxford University Press. Online at: http://www.oxforddictionaries.com/definition/english/management

tells his or her team what to do, using strict processes, manuals and protocols, perhaps from a hands-off approach or perhaps a controlling micromanagement style. The average manager often does not consider the futures, opinions or feelings of staff, expecting them to get on and do it. A leader brings inspiration and charisma, which staff will know well and respect. A manager may be introvert, staying behind a desk with a perceived unapproachable closed-door policy.

For many of us who learned our business skills in a big organisation, we attended management courses which taught us how to motivate, communicate and above all control the activities that we were responsible for. We were measured by our degree of achievement, or overachievement, of our given objectives. Our rewards were calculated on this factor. Our leadership skills were rarely honed through courses. Due to employers failing to invest sufficiently in the development of their people, and inefficiently, it is highly likely that your skills were developed by personal experience, self-development and circumstantial need. That said we all looked up the ladder within the organisation to the board members and particularly the CEO for leadership and we all knew, instinctively, when we were not getting it.

It is also not uncommon for large organisations to have a culture expecting you to deliver, behave and manage in a certain way when the top leadership to whom you report does not lead by example or practise what they preach. Have you suffered in the past from working for someone more senior but who knows, contributes and cares less than you do about what needs to be done to perform well and support your employer? We have! Think carefully about how you can avoid the employees in your small or medium-sized business from feeling the same way about your leadership. If you lead by example, and manage less frequently but appropriately, then your team will be more motivated and more productive for you. A positive example of when management is required over leadership could be in a disciplinary example whereby human resources, and legal protocols are very important to avoid a burdensome employment tribunal.

Now that we are in full control of our own businesses, if we are to apply the criteria of our past experiences, do we see ourselves as leaders or managers? And what do we aspire to be? What support and development do you need to encounter to be the effective, respected and successful business leader you want to be?

In the first instance, the fact that you now have your own business demonstrates some innate leadership qualities. You have a vision with a plan and direction in which to fulfil that goal. But can you take others with you on that journey? This is not just about getting those that work for you to come along but also those that you work with internally and externally to your firm – including your supportive family, close friends, investors, suppliers and customers. They are all (and should be treated as) very important stakeholders in your success.

You will also know that it will never be enough to just have the vision or talk about it. A course will have to be steered very closely and corrections made to avoid being blown off course by external events. The crew will have to be trained in their tasks to ensure that the engine room is maintained to propel your vessel and be able to respond to the high winds, storms and rough seas that you will inevitably meet along the way. And somebody needs to be directing and coordinating those tasks to make sure that the right thing is happening at the right time.

To continue the analogy you may have the vision to go the other route and you must have the credibility to convince others to support your quest, and the charisma to enrol a crew who will work with you effectively. That is a successful leader. But can you navigate the ship in the right direction, keep discipline amongst the ranks, weather the storms, take the disappointment of finding America rather than your original objective and then recognise the advantages?

If you have been a manager then you need to change your workplace paradigm. The two hats have to be worn appropriately. You are still required to wear the management hat and communicate, motivate and control, but you also have to be confident and comfortable in the leadership hat to:

- aspire,
- inspire, and
- require.

Chapter 12

People Development

It is not enough to employ someone into your business, train them to do the job and then just leave them to get on with it. Things change, people change, business conditions change, technology changes, personal aspirations change, competitive threats change, the law changes – the list goes on and your business needs to respond to all of these. One of the surest ways of meeting these changing situations is, to quote a well-known accreditation, 'Invest in people.'

Another frequently quoted gem is 'Work on your business, not in your business.' Well, if that is to be true, and it needs to be, then you need capable and able people working in the business to allow you to work on the business. Building your winning team means recruiting for the skills you lack and the responsibilities you should be delegating to work on the business. Surround yourself with people you feel are great both in your business and your personal life too. In doing this, whoever is working in the business needs to be consistently up to the task so that you are not forever looking over their shoulder or constantly checking their work because you do not have the confidence to let them onto a longer lead. Writing from experience, people are generally keen to do a good job and become expert in what they do. I accept there are exceptions to this, but you wouldn't be employing these exceptions anyway – would you?

You will find little, if any, resistance to training people. Well-trained and continually developing people are satisfied at work, which leads to more concentration on the job rather than finding things wrong with it. Also think about other forms of retaining good people and driving the best performance from your team. People who are continually trained well and motivated by rewards tailored to their individual preferences require far less supervision in achieving greater results. They can be relied upon to support and promote your business. The point to bear in mind is that if your reason for providing training is always because the employee is not up to the task this will not present the most motivating of reasons for them to take part and engage fully. Personal development is a positive and should be sold as such, alongside additional incentives and direction to drive the right behaviours and actions. For example, someone motivated by work-life balance and time off work is unlikely to be motivated by large cash bonuses. The chance for that person to earn extra days off for exceeding targets is far more likely to make them your most loyal team member.

People development is not just about technical job skills. Consider people skills such as communication, influence, personal effectiveness, motivational leadership, interpersonal skills and team building. For example, people can become more supportive of your business if they become better team players, have a more confident telephone manner or speak another language. This is not an exhaustive list, but it attempts to demonstrate that by developing your people as people and not just as business machines your business will become more effective and thus more attractive to your customers. People will be able and motivated to step up and perform. That should be encouraged as much as possible because it will allow you to work on the business and get a better home/work balance.

It has been said many times that 'If I train people they will only leave.' The counter point is that if they are good people they will leave if you don't train them. And if they are not good people they will stay, and you will be forever working in the business. In addition, if they were developed and incentivised correctly to stay and develop within your business long term, then why would they even consider leaving?

Chapter 13

Cash is King

No, we are not going to present you with a picture of a lion with a caption. The point is, however, that without available cash (liquidity) you are sunk (bankrupt, scuttled, insolvent, bust). Profits in themselves will not keep you afloat. Cash flow is about timing as well as total income minus total expenditure and getting a positive number. It is a false hope for the big feast into the future when there is no food on the table every day up until that point. And this time next year we will not be millionaires unless cash is tightly controlled on what is coming in, and when, and what is going out, and when.

If you have any doubts about this then try an exercise for yourself. Allocate yourself a budget over at least a month for something you enjoy; let's say cigarettes, or coffee at the railway station, or a pint after work. Let us assume (and never try this at home – it makes an Ass out of U and Me) that your budget is £3 per day with 22 working days per month. Your total monthly budget is £66. Now allocate that budget into four cash receipts of £16.50 to be paid in on 1st, 8th, 15th and 22nd. Now work to that budget without borrowing from somewhere else. You have to exist on what you have, even if you decide to buy an item for a friend. If you do borrow then charge a 10% interest on the amount to be paid from your next income and measure the effect. That is what is happening with your business.

You can even try receiving your weekly income a day or two late, just like your customers and suppliers do. How many daily items did you have to forego to remain in the black? This represents the number of customers or suppliers you will have disappointed through your lack of cash, or the number of invoices that would have been late in being paid. How much credit control time and borrowing cost are you causing your suppliers if you pay them late? How would you feel if your customers did it to you? If you care for others, and have a conscience, then pay within the terms you agree or sign up to. The old saying 'treat others as you expect to be treated' resonates here.

Now try and not receive a weekly income at all. Are you getting withdrawal symptoms or is the need so great that you have to borrow again? Remember, when you borrow your costs have risen by 10% but your budget hasn't.

Even if you borrow from your other pocket or purse, a knock on effect is being created and your available cash is being squeezed whilst your potential need for external financing is increasing.

Please do not take this as a patronising exercise. Many companies have been put into administration or liquidation because of lack of cash and not lack of profitability. Many times that cash flow pressure was brought on by another party, customers paying late, or suppliers causing delays. Timing is everything, especially so when you are asked to produce a cash flow forecast. If you have a cash flow forecast, then you have a diet, which is keeping you alive. You might be very wary after a while but you are still independent. There are no free food parcels in business and when you do get to the feast, you can enjoy it knowing that your debts have been paid and it is not your last request before your existence is taken away from you.

Chapter 14

Releasing the Cash in Your Business

Having established that cash control is a crucial element in your business operation, it is worth examining alternative ways that you can improve your cash position. This is not an impossible task and we know of finance specialists who consistently deliver 30% increase in available cash within the first three months of engaging with client companies.

The first attack is to look at the money that is owed to you. How much of that is more than one week late from the date it was due? This is money that belongs with you and should have been with you at least a week ago. Do you chase for this money, or are you too busy to call the customer and ask for payment? Maybe you are reticent about chasing your client as you are fearful of harassing them. Granted, sometimes this is difficult to gain confidence in doing, but it does not have to be done in such a tone that a relationship is destroyed by it. And if you are concerned that having sold to the customer it is a different relationship in chasing for payment then get somebody who is not in sales to do the call. In fact I think that this is a basic discipline in a business – separate sales from credit control. The reason for the late payment may be that you have not presented your invoice in the right way, to the right person, or in the right timeframe. Get to know your customers' payment cycles. They may only do one payment run a month, in which case if you miss their submission date then you will be waiting another month for your money. Get into sync with their cycle and ensure that your invoice is submitted before the cut-off date and then you will have every reason to question a non-payment.

You can also look at invoices which are regular. For example, you have a customer who effectively pays you a retainer every month. If this is the case why not raise your invoice at the beginning of the month rather than after the actual service has been delivered? Linking this to the above paragraph could bring that payment in more than four weeks earlier than previously was the case.

The second attack is to look at the money you spend – both in terms of spending and timing. We are in no way advocating making late payments but if a supplier is making available payment terms to you then make use of them. If payment is due in 30 days then that is when payment should be made – not at day 1.

As far as costs are concerned you should be examining every cost element in your business. Again we are not advocating going for the cheapest supplier because there could well be a level of service or quality within that price that would be lost by going with a cheaper supplier. But if you can get the same level of service for less cost then why not change supplier, although let your existing supplier know why before you leave. If you are a good customer, you may be able to influence improved terms with the existing provider. Take a look at your costs for everything and also decide if you are getting good value for money for photocopying, utility bills, bank charges, professional services fees, equipment hire and lease. Get the best deal that you can – every time, all of the time.

One last word on the cash issue. We all look at our fixed costs and have been taught that as long as fixed costs are covered then you can survive. Let us be clear that the world has changed – there is no such thing as a fixed cost. If you don't believe us, then pretend that you have not been successful and are looking at coming to an agreement with your creditors. You will be discussing what percentage of the bill you will pay back and it will be less than 100%. So why not take a similar view while you are successful? There is an old saying 'In life you get what you deserve. In business you get what you negotiate.'

Chapter 15

You Can't Control Everything

However much we like to think that we are in complete control and have everything in its place, we are deluding ourselves. There is so much in the business environment that can change rapidly, sometimes without any notice, which will upset our plans and have the potential to ruin the business. Use this chapter to make some 'what if scenario' plans. What measures can you implement to prepare or mitigate risk in unforeseen circumstances?

Some years ago I lived next door to a small holding where my neighbour had the idea of starting a business rearing pheasants to sell to estates to enlarge their stocks of birds for shooting parties. In his first year he did extremely well and made a very healthy profit, and then set out his stall for the following year. However, year two was not the same as year one and by the end of year two he had to liquidate the company. What was the difference between the two years? The market was the same size and he had an increased demand from customers compared to year one. Prices were slightly higher in the second year. Unit costs were also on a par. So what was the difference? The answer is: the weather. In year one the weather had been very kind with a mild spring and a gorgeously warm summer. This meant that the business had a good hatching rate and heating costs were low due to the high ambient temperatures. However, in year two it was a cold, wet spring and a usual British summer. This reduced hatching success and increased the heating bills considerably in order to maintain the chicks at sustainable temperatures. The result was a reduced supply against increased demand, a significant increase in costs, and a realisation of the true costs of the business.

In this example it is clear that the weather was not in any way under the control of the business. The cash was. The outcome from year one was treated as normal, even though the weather was unusual. Rather than the healthy profit from year one being used to cushion the likely outcome in year two with an average summer, it was treated as usual and the plans were set for year two on the best-case scenario.

This may seem an obvious set of circumstances for the business but it does demonstrate that while the weather was outside of the influence of the business owner he could have taken it into account by planning in line with the usual British summer and budgeting accordingly or setting aside a cash buffer earned in the good year.

There is a plethora of other unmanageable elements in the mix ranging from taxation to supplier insolvency. In each of them there is little that you can do to change the impact, but once you recognise them and put them actively into your plan, you can accommodate them with counteractions to keep your business on track, even if you have to change tactics in order to avoid being sunk by an incoming perfect storm.

Our colleague, Richard Weaver, uses the analogy of a fried egg to produce a tool for managing the manageable and mitigating the unmanageable. You put the manageable into the yoke and the unmanageable into the white, then literally cut and throw the white away. It is a compelling model and an essential business tool for any serious and ambitious business owner/entrepreneur.

Chapter 16

Quality, Targeted Business Development

Like new-build houses, the titles given to jobs seem to corrupt the original meaning of the description – what is an executive home anyway? That is certainly what has happened to business development. Sales has become a dirty word, being replaced by business development. We didn't see that in our edition of Roget's Thesaurus and that is because, in the true sense, they are not synonymous. More accurately, they are complimentary activities along the line of building a strong customer base that will buy repeatedly.

Business development is the two-way conduit from marketing to sales. If business development does not target the same audience as marketing then the brand will become weakened, prospective customers will become confused as to what the company is and what it does and sales will have an impossible job to close deals. From this it can be appreciated that business development is an activity of its own, but cannot exist in isolation. It is an important cog in the marketing and sales machine.

Business development is the activity that builds upon the communication message broadcast by marketing. Marketing will be targeting the audience relevant to the company's offering and will aim to interest as many potential customers as possible, maximising audience capture for the company prospect/sales funnel. Business development will further target that audience and through building close relationships will understand how the company can best serve those customers and provide sales with the sharpened appropriate tools with which to fully engage, pull the prospect down through the sales funnel and convert a potential sale into a real one.

Business development will use skills that are different to marketing and sales, yet are complimentary. It would be very unusual for one person to be able to perform all three functions with the same level of skill and success. There are generally three different personality types – one for each of the activities. People can cross the boundaries and, as already said, the line is a continuum so some individuals can spread their personality and skills across the areas. The important thing to distinguish is what needs to be achieved in each area and not what can be done by one individual in each.

So what is quality, targeted business development? The quality is dictated by the appropriateness of the message to the audience and driven by hitting the right targets. Just take one example. We know of a company that makes high-quality bespoke products and their marketing material emphasises this. However, their business development is not concentrated on customers and intermediaries within this high-end population. Rather than being like a sniper and aiming at the bullseye, a blunderbuss is used to hit whatever comes into range. The result is that they get into sales discussions where they are selling on price and not on bespoke high quality. This then convinces them that to compete they need to move down market. However, to do this they need to change their ethos and operating model. If, on the other hand, they were to only spend their time talking to the people who would want and can afford their level of product, expertise, skill and customer service, then the conversation would be about what they do, not how their price compares to competitors. More than that, it would be about what they do really well and for which there is very little competition. What is happening with this company is that they have a loyal customer base that has used them for many years, but potential new customers are in the low price bracket.

Our advice to all companies is to focus on and do what you do really well. Understand your ideal customer base and decide if that constitutes a viable marketplace considered alongside other factors:

- the size of your prospect client base,
- market conditions, and
- the capability of your competition.

If it does, then:

- line up your marketing communication,
- target your business development activity to building quality relationships with the right customer and intermediary base in the way that accounts for the preferences in how they might want to be communicated to. Then,
- reap the rewards by winning sales from this nurtured group of clients and introducers.

Chapter 17

Growing Pains

We have all had them at some time, or even times, in our lives and if your business is healthy then it too will go through growing pains. There is nothing to worry about. It is more of a worry if you don't go through this at various times as this will mean that your business is under-nourished or has a growth deficiency disorder. Either way you will need to do the right things about each of them in order to survive and flourish.

Your business should grow in three ways:

1. It will sell more and generate more revenue.
2. It will grow in the number of people required to support the business (and with the right people at that).
3. It will grow in value.

As the owner of the business you will need to identify where you are on the growth path with each of these and know if you are on course to be a fully-developed, mature being, or will you have vitamin deficiencies and stunted growth.

Managing your growth is a strategic activity. It is not just operational and it cannot be allowed to happen from the bottom up. You are likely to have started your business from small beginnings – maybe just you. As sales grew you needed to employ help and so you took on people to do the work that you could not handle or did not desire to do. After a while your recruitment, probably, was driven by someone you had hired who then screamed louder than anyone else that they needed more resources. This is what we mean by bottom up. As we have said, this is a strategic activity and should happen from the top down. If it does not happen top down then your development will be unbalanced. You will find many employees doing non-income generating work, non-development work, and growth will be slowed.

As in life you will need to grow with your business. You cannot stay in short trousers all of your life. At the start of your business you were concerned with:

- Product
- Selling
- Income

So at this stage your focus was on resource and having the capability to deliver. After a while you will have changed your focus to organisation and function in order to have the right people in the right place doing the right things – so a move to strategy. Now at maturity you will continue to concentrate on strategic issues but rather than looking at purely revenue streams you will be concerned with growing the value of your company to enable you to increase your options on exit and retirement.

Each of these stages will take a different skill set to lead your business in the right direction. If you do not recognise where you are on the growth path then you will be living on a poor diet with the consequences to come in later years (or maybe months). However, if you nourish your business appropriately then fitness will prevail, and development with future good health will have you relishing your old age.

Chapter 18

Move with the Times

When we see a company that is proud to announce in its signage that it was established in the last millennium we can understand their pride in their achievement at still being in business after thirty, forty, or even fifty years. After all, how many companies of any size can make that boast?

This is rarely through gifted good fortune and luck. What it usually demonstrates is that the company has adapted to changing: trends, conditions of business, regulations and customer expectations to remain a supplier of choice with a product or service that customers will pay money to receive.

Adaptability should not be underestimated. What we need to remind ourselves is that change is continuous and ever quickening. Take, for example, the recorded music industry. It took over 50 years from the time recording was invented to the mass production and sale of recorded music. At that time 78rpm, around for over 30 years, was replaced by 33rpm living alongside the 45rpm single. These formats co-existed for 25 years until the introduction of the compact disc. And how long before downloading became the vogue? Alongside these changes we have witnessed the demise of the retail record store and as recently as 2012, we saw a bastion of the retail sector, HMV, collapse. A change too far for HMV or a lack of response to a changing industry?

Another example is the average high street. Can you remember when the high street was the place to shop? It had variety, experts and competition. What it also had was an expensive cost base and no space for all of those newfangled cars, which everybody insisted on travelling about in. More often than not, every high street is now identified by short lease charity shops and pound shops with a very few special interest shops that provide enough attraction to get their customers to venture from the mall and explore the parade.

The point is true of whatever industry in which you are engaged. A plumber has had to adopt new materials and techniques, an electrician new regulations and technology, and the refuse collection has changed the shape of bins and the frequency of collections. No industry is exempt – not even the nostalgia and memorabilia markets.

Coronation Street has been around for over 50 years and, with the exception of William Roache, has made countless changes to characters, storylines and sets in order to retain its appeal to its audience who by now is probably in its third or fourth generation.

That is the message for all businesses – remain relevant to your customers. Be very aware of not only your product life cycle, but also your business environment. Know which of your product lines are the most popular and sell like hotcakes, but also know those that have passed their 'Best Before' date and those new lines that show all the promise to be the 'best thing since sliced bread'. And when you have, then take the necessary action. Sentimentality or complacency will leave you with fewer and fewer customers as they change their habits and their desires. Loyalty will give you some cushion but not in perpetuity. Change with the times and instead of coming down the curve from product and market maturity, take actions to make it an S curve upwards and take advantage of the slowness of your competitors.

Chapter 19

4D Networking

We know what you are asking 'Do I need special spectacles to see this 4D approach?' The answer is simply, no, but you do need to understand how to approach networking in this way and why it is different from the traditional modus operandi.

The traditional 2D method of networking is to:

- attend a networking event armed with your business cards,
- talk to as many people as you can, and
- sell your product as hard as you can to everyone you meet.

You may set yourself a ratio, maybe 10:1, that is one piece of potential business for every ten conversations. The thing is that you may be in the wrong place for your product and your ratio is umpteen to nil. On the other hand where you are successful and get a positive lead the next thing you have to do is to repeat the exercise at another event to obtain the next customer. A life on the networking treadmill will ensue.

You can develop this model to the 3D approach. In this method you develop relationships with businesses that can refer clients on an on-going basis to you, and you to them. Strange as it may seem, your bank manager is potentially a good networking partner. If they are any good, then your accountant and solicitor equally so and, dare I mention it – your business advisor (excuse the bias when we write). In this way your networking efforts are concentrated on mutually beneficial non-competing, complimentary referral contacts and not going all out for the direct to prospect customer sale. In the 2D approach you will have introduced yourself to someone who operates in a totally different business galaxy to you and you would have moved on quickly as there was no chance of a sale. However, their network may have included prime customers for you. Did you stay long enough to find this out and get to know them? A lost opportunity, or two, or three, or… You get the idea.

4D networking takes this even a stage further. By building strong, long-term relationships with your referrers, you will also build a trust so that when they refer someone to you they know that their customer will get good service from you and this reinforces their reputation. The same is true when you refer one of your customers/contacts to them. The other difference is that rather than just introducing new business to each other, you can build the network by introducing people across your network that could benefit from one another. This will reinforce your reputation as an introducer, provided your introductions are between like-minded people with complimentary aspirations, purpose, values and interests who can benefit from your introduction. We also call these approaches strategic partnership or collaborative cross-pollination of business friends, client bases and networks.

The important element to recognise in the 4D approach is that it has to form a key element in your business development strategy. You need to understand who your key relationships should be with and aim for those people. Make sure they are like-minded and reliable. Firing a shot in the air and hoping that it will hit somebody is a waste of your ammunition and time. You will know from your business strategy who your ideal market segment contains and who the important customers are. You need to translate that into who do these people necessarily talk to in going about their private or business lives. It is these people who will open doors to your marketplace. There are plenty of research statistics to prove that if you integrate your customers across your quality, trusted network of business friends and strategic suppliers then they become sticker (retained), buy more from you (cross sales or upselling) and are also more likely to refer you to others.

Reputation is a crucial element in being successful in this method. Build a reputation of being accurate, sensitive to compatibility, and convergence and you will have a reputation that is enviable. But one word of warning – do not be naïve. If you are referring to somebody who never returns back to you, doesn't say thanks and doesn't follow up promptly, then face up to it – they are the wrong partner and you should get out of the one-way street.

As a final note, with 4D networking being an integral part of your overall strategy and business development strategy you will be targeted. What you will also discover is that you will do less networking but more effective and rewarding relationship, partnership and reputation building. The volume and quality of prospects, partnerships and potential employees will increase positively too – all wanting to be a part of your high-quality team, brand and network.

Forget the special spectacles; just improve your peripheral vision by thinking outside the box with your overall approach to business. They say 'surround yourself with great people', 'build your winning team'. Such applies to your customer base, suppliers (including advisory parties), collaborative partnerships, co-directors, personal friendships, life partner and employees!

Chapter 20

Be Loyal, Be Reliable and Be Trusted

This chapter and its topic is really a complimentary extension of the important concept in chapter 21. During your business life you will recommend friends, acquaintances and business contacts to one another and, hopefully, they will do the same for you. But ask yourself this, how many times have you been referred to someone and they turn out to be a poor supplier or even an unreliable person? And how many times have you just referred someone for the sake of it without thinking about the appropriateness of the referral. These are critical questions, and bad referrals are bad business. Yes, bad business. Full stop.

On the other hand, good referrals are good business and will help you to develop your customer base and your reputation for referrals that really work. In this way, others will recommend you to more people and make effective use of referrals that you make to them. By doing this you can directly build your reputation and do it vicariously through the dependability of your referrals. Simple principle, but is it simple in reality?

If I refer someone to another business professional I want to know that they will receive the service they require, at least to the standards that I expect. After all, they are my customer, even though I have referred them on. If the referral doesn't work then my reputation is tarnished for having made the referral. Similarly, the person receiving the referral will be wary of my future referrals if the person referred turns out to be a time-waster for them.

We have touched on 4D networking and how that can generate a large number of referrals from your network. But your network is like your sales. One disappointed customer will share their disappointment with, on average, eleven others, while one satisfied customer will tell a few trusted friends. A happy person referred on will tell a few but an unhappy one will tell everybody. Again, like your sales, a new long-term, quality referrer will take a lot more effort to achieve than having the reliability of existing partners. What is worse than the sales situation is that your network is smaller and more closely connected than your customer base and so word is likely to spread further and faster. Also think about the social networking media – do you want a public bad reputation?

You will soon get to know your network. After all, you have chosen everyone who is a member. You should know their strengths, weaknesses, abilities, capacities and values. Only make referrals where all of these elements are a match. In addition, make sure it's not just about business too. So many people skip the interpersonal element – crucial in rapport building and establishing the relationship. Where are they from? What do they like to do when they are not in the office building their business? What common ground do you share in the form of family and hobbies?

As in all things, a good reputation and solid relationships are won over time by consistently being good. That reputation or relationship is easily and quickly lost by even just one wrong event. Be conscious of the referrals you make and build a stronger reputation – that reputation will seep into the view for other areas of your business delivery too.

Chapter 21

Advanced Stakeholder Management

Don't get dismissive of who are the stakeholders in your business, and certainly work hard to maintain and build their commitment to your business and success. To do this you will need to go further than the standard 'keep everyone informed' model. Advanced stakeholder management requires an energetic, engaging approach and not a passive 'If I must!' disregard.

Think about all of those that have a stake in the success of your business rather than confining yourself to your shareholder agreement and your bank manager who granted you the overdraft and the loan. If you do this then the list will expand to include suppliers and customers to name a few. But, why are they stakeholders in my business? Because their success depends upon you and vice versa. Of course this is not true if you change suppliers with every order, or do nothing to nurture loyal customers.

Examine the role of your suppliers. They can be of more help to you than supplying goods on time and giving you good prices. A major motor manufacturer produced their cars with a different colour roof to the body. There was obviously a major paint masking job to be done on every car before going through the paint spraying process. The internal engineers worked on this problem for months without finding a solution which would fit with the operation process time, i.e. it was taking far too long for the masking. The manufacturer then approached the paint supplier who provided a solution that bettered the required process time and ensured the right quality of finish every time. The savings to the manufacturer were immense and made with every car.

This would not have been possible if the relationship with the supplier had been adversarial. As it is, the supplier has a customer that is loyal to their product and spends big bucks with them continually. The manufacturer has an efficient and effective solution allowing them to maintain their desired colour option schemes at a competitive price = happy customers all round!

It is a similar situation with your customers. If you think about it you probably do this already, but mainly to beat the competition away from that customer and not to build that mutually beneficial relationship with your customer. Think of the example above. Would you have provided the solution? Or would you have seen more profit in the paint that would be paid for but wasted?

You should even consider your current stakeholders. Take the example of your bank manager. How often do you have a conversation with your bank manager about your business plans, funding needs and management of surpluses? Probably, never. What is more likely is that you talk to your bank manager when you need something. Even more likely is when that something is urgent. What is also likely is that the answer you have got used to is, no. What if you were to change that relationship to sharing your plans and tribulations, so that the urgent need can be responded to in the right context – that of your real business position and not a snapshot of impending trouble. Would that get you what you need and prevent the predictable problem? Probably, yes.

Advanced stakeholder management, therefore, is about managing all of the people around you to obtain the best results for the overall business. Not everything is a battle – cooperative working and mutual benefit brings significant advantages over and over again. But don't be naïve – choose your friends wisely.

Chapter 22

Strategic Partnerships: Two Heads Are Better Than One

It is often said that two heads are better than one, and whilst this is true of problem solving, it can also be an extremely effective way to do business.

Collaborating intracompany, between departments or segments has long been used in large corporates in order to increase wallet share amongst their client base, but a relatively overlooked strategy, especially at small business level, is intercompany collaboration or strategic partnerships.

A strategic partnership, 'a formal alliance between two commercial enterprises', can be used in a multitude of ways, including, but not limited to:

- boosting revenues,
- delivering more effective marketing, or
- reaching more prospects by both parties sharing their client base.

No matter what your small business is, it is unlikely to be everything to everyone, and partnering with an organisation that offers a complementary product or service can allow both companies to exploit their own strengths, whilst benefitting from the support that a strategic partnership offers. This can also work for companies within the same industry sector – competitive friendships. How many of your alleged competitors actually have a capacity or desire for new clients? How many of them really do target the same size or type of clients as you?

> Win, Win, Win...

In many industries, we have witnessed larger firms who specialise in supplying medium corporate clients, and they regularly get approached by clients who are too small. What happens to those? They turn them away! The same is true in reverse. We have seen many small companies taking on business clients whose demands are too big or specialist for their true delivery capabilities. Do they turn them away? No. They take them on, and you guessed it, they overtrade, mess up and cause more problems than they would have if they had been honest and said 'thanks, but no' in the first place. On the contrary, for example, if a small firm specialising in providing IT consultancy services to businesses with less than 20 employees, partners with a larger IT firm specialising in medium-sized firms (20 staff or more), then both firms can refer their undesired clients to each other, and perhaps even share the revenue by passing on a percentage of success fees. In this scenario, both same sector companies benefit in multiple ways, and more importantly, the customers get a far better service at the right time with less cost and hassle.

> Buy, Buy, Buy...

Buying groups have been around for a long time, offering their members the opportunity to purchase their stock with the benefit of the increased buying power not available to an individual entity outside of the group.

This is a perfect example of an effective strategic partnership at work.

All companies within the buying group have a common goal, to reduce their procurement costs, and by partnering together within the group, they are all able to achieve this goal, at no detriment to the individual members.

Utilising strategic partnerships to reduce costs need not be stock purchase related however, and can work just as effectively in the service industry.

A website design could form a partnership with a PR, a social media outsource consultancy and/or a branding company, embarking on a joint marketing campaign offering all services as a 'full package' offering, winning business for both companies, whilst sharing the advertising cost. With such an approach, maybe it isn't about new external advertising. Maybe it is about cross-fertilising services across each other's existing client and prospect databases.

In another example, a PR firm pitches its services to a prospective customer and does not win the business. In an alternative approach to the latter example, a PR firm opens its pitch by fact-finding and getting to know the exact needs and wants of the prospective client. They realise that the client's more immediate priority is the website design and rebranding. Kicking their strategic partnership network into action, the PR firm brings in the web design outfit and the brand consultants who embark on a 3-month project for the prospect. In month 2, the client brings in the PR firm to plan the launch of the new website and the rebrand. Ironically, the PR campaign will be more successful with the improved brand and website, so the client will be happier, moving into a long-term, retained relationship, and referring their business friends!

One example of a successful strategic partnership is that between Facebook, and the music streaming service, Spotify. With an audience of over 970 million[6], Facebook provides a huge opportunity for other companies to tap into. Spotify did just this, offering users the option

6 Twitter Statistics, 2014. *Statistic Brain*. Online at: http://www.statisticbrain.com/twitter-statistics/

to link their Spotify account to their Facebook account. Spotify found that users who did this were three times more likely to become paid subscribers than those who didn't. Overall, not a bad result!

> Me, Me, Me...

The challenge for many businesses when contemplating the formation of a strategic partnership is to move away from the notion that it should only benefit one party.

A strategic partnership should be exactly that, a partnership, a joining of two, or even more, businesses that can provide between them the same level of commitment to deliver growth opportunities for all involved – each partner, each other and most importantly, their respective clients. It's that win, win, win philosophy again.

Business can be a selfish pursuit, not because it is necessarily that way inherently, but because the high level of focus and long hours that are required can often cause the business owner to spend too much time in the business instead of on the business, thus stifling growth.

Strategic partnerships can be found in the most unlikely of places, as much between perceived competitors as those offering complementary products or services.

Apple, for example, took a $150m investment from Microsoft in 1997 in order to take the company to the next level, and few people now would criticise that decision, no matter how controversial it seemed at the time.

The benefits offered by strategic partnerships are too great to ignore and, provided the partnership is executed correctly, such collaboration could be the difference between a good company and a great one.

> So What Next?

Any potential strategic partnership has to be carefully considered before agreements are made, however, they can provide unparalleled revenue growth and brand awareness opportunities if executed correctly.

Consider what products or services your business offers, and then put yourself in your customers' shoes; what else might your customers need in addition to what you can provide them?

Do you own a restaurant with clients who often visit a local wine bar after having dinner? Strike up a strategic partnership offering to promote the wine bar when you present the restaurant bill in exchange for a commission on revenue generated. Alternatively, or in addition, get the wine bar to provide a discount voucher at your restaurant to be used within the next week. Again, the wine bar owners could receive a success fee for that, but the real value is that if the clients do return to your restaurant to use that voucher, then your restaurant staff will be driving them back to your wine bar rather than one of your local competitors!

Are you an accountant with a client base who would benefit from legal expertise? Seek out a strategic partnership with a law firm and offer an enhanced small business package. Maybe your accountancy firm also has clients who need business growth coaching and staff skills training? A business coach can provide that service, making your clients more likely to stay in business with you as their accountant, and they'll most certainly become a bigger business needing more of your services. With you being the one to connect them with the additional service providers, they are eternally grateful, and more likely to refer you to their other successful business friends who need a better, seemingly more proactive and caring accountant. Don't forget other positive knock-on effects through the business coach and the law firm whom you referred to your client. It's hard winning new clients these days and they are very grateful that you gifted them with a great client and will work doubly hard to return the favour when their clients need a change of accountant! That's right, from matching the needs of a client to the services of a non-competing external provider you could quite easily receive one, two, three or more new clients in return! Try it.

No matter the size of your business, or the sector you operate in, the possibilities are endless provided the strategic partnership is well thought out, commercially viable and beneficial to both parties involved.

As the saying goes, two heads are indeed better than one.

Chapter 23

Plan, Review, Plan, Review, Over and Over Again

> Performance Management: A Model Process

Performance management is an essential practice for corporate organisations, but is regularly overlooked by SMEs, often having a significantly detrimental impact on the business. Managing your employee's performance is a critical element in ensuring the on-going success of your business, and in maintaining an engaged, motivated workforce.

> Time to Prioritise

There are two key challenges that prevent small business owners from effectively managing their employee's performance, but if you are serious about growing your business, these challenges need to be overcome.

Performance management cannot be done quickly. It demands that time is spent assessing performance, considering how performance can be improved and discussing with your employee's how these improvements can be implemented.

Whilst your time is precious as a small business owner, you need to prioritise the matters that will move your business forward. Effective performance management is one of those most important matters.

> A Model Process

Once the time for dedicating to performance management has been set aside, it has to be approached in a structured manner that objectively evaluates performance, and sets out the clear objectives which will measure improvement.

A common model used when conducting performance management reviews is the performance management cycle. This model can be applied to any employee and or department, provided that all stages of the cycle are in place.

> Plan

Set aside some time to plan how you are going to approach the performance management review. Consider the key areas for discussion, what metrics you are going to measure, and prepare some suggestions for how performance can be improved. Make sure you ask the employee:

- how they feel it is going,
- what do they think they can do to improve performance, and
- what support, if any, do they require to achieve such results?

> Act

Work alongside your employee to implement any changes required to successfully deliver the objectives set. Supporting your employee is absolutely critical, and will allow you to quickly act if further changes are required.

> Monitor

In the same way that you should regularly monitor the profit you are making on your sales, you need to monitor the progress being made by your employees following the implementation of any changes. Performance management should be an on-going exercise to support your employees, not something that only gets covered during an annual review.

> Review

Depending on the timescales agreed during the initial meeting, the review stage should involve another, structured meeting with your employee, discussing the progress that has been made and evaluating their performance against the agreed objectives.

It is at this stage that the performance management cycle begins again.

Chapter 24

Quality

Quality has to drive everything that you do in your business. Quality is no longer a differentiator; instead it is the price of entry. If your business does not meet your customers' expectations of: quality in product, service, accessibility, communication, advertising, supply and customer support then you do not have a sustainable business.

Think about quality as part of your marketing mix. It will help to put the product, the price, any promotion, and the place into context. For example, if you are located in the centre of Knightsbridge, London and your customers are all well heeled then your price will be at the high end, your product will also be at the high end, your level of service will be second to none, and your promotions will resonate with these customers' values and expectations. If, on the other hand, you are located in Tower Hamlets and your customers are low income families then your price will be low, your product will meet their needs and affordability, whilst your levels of service will, again, meet with their expectations when price is the driving consideration, and promotions will resonate with different values and expectations. You cannot deliver the highest quality and charge the lowest price.

It is a question often asked: what is the price of quality? In simple terms, the real cost is found when quality is not present because that is when your customers desert you in favour of a competitor who offers them better value for money and who, at the same time, meets their expectations. Be very clear. You cannot offer Rolls-Royce quality at Trabant prices even if your customers have champagne tastes and beer bottle pockets. The equation has to balance.

Also be aware that quality, and the cost of quality, are not static features. If you are a new manufacturing company then quality will improve with experience and the cost will actually decrease with that same experience. In this situation, if you have got the equation right for your customer base at the beginning then experience will bring you competitive advantage as you are able to deliver higher quality with no cost increase. On the other hand, do not let increases in material prices dictate the level of quality. A decrease in quality, for the same price, will be felt by the customer, and unless you are in a monopoly position, it will result in lost sales.

Quality, and with it reliability of product and service, have to form the basis of your company's offering to your customers. Do not get confused when you see a promotion that seems too good to be true. Even Harrods have a sale, but remember that this is for a specific reason and over a very limited period of time. Overall, the worldwide reputation of the store is kept intact but for a short time ageing stock is disposed of, customers, who otherwise would only dream of buying from there, can fulfil that dream and the company continues for the remainder of the year working to a formula that delivers to its true customer base and the company objectives.

All companies can be like Harrods – not all sale signs mean a failing business. If it is because of distress then the signs were there long before the sale.

Chapter 25

Process is Sacrosanct – Discuss

A lot of importance has been made about working to process over the last twenty years, and much of it prompted by achieving coveted quality standards recognition. Many companies that we have worked with have then become rigid about the process and demand compliance from all. At an individual level this can translate into an excuse for not meeting customers' (both internal and external) requirements or expectations.

We hold the view that processes are an essential discipline for a business, but not a cage from which there is no escape. They provide the tramlines for consistency and the ability to continuously look at the business to see how things can be improved. They also provide the marker for when everything goes pear-shaped to see:

- how far you have deviated,
- what needs to be done to get back on track, and
- what changes need to be made to stop that occurrence happening in the future.

Don't get us wrong. We are not proposing here that processes are not worth the paper they are written on and should be dispensed with. On the contrary, defined, well-thought-through, tried and tested, and robust processes are what give us confidence in our ability to deliver consistent results. What we are suggesting is that processes should be used as a tool to provide consistency and repeatability but also to identify waste and eliminate it. Processes themselves can and should be improved.

> What a Waste!

We are never surprised by how narrow a view some businesses have on what is waste. Measuring scrap and rework are obvious examples, but what about the inefficiencies in the way that the business is conducted? We give here a few examples:

1. In the NHS a senior nurse needed to obtain a report from another hospital some 80 miles away. The report was needed the next day. The solution was to arrange for the report to be made available for collection and then for that senior nurse to travel, personally, by car the following day to collect the report. This had the result that a frontline member of staff spent a whole working day travelling, claiming mileage at a rate of £0.40 per mile and not being available to deliver patient care during that absence.

Where was the waste in this? Internal procedures did not allow for the use of a courier without approval, which would be 48 hours to obtain. You will have come to your own conclusions already but procedures were followed.

Even so, there were other alternatives. The NHS has a secure email service for the transfer of confidential information. Would this not have been an effective and efficient way of obtaining the required report?

2. A manufacturing company, with ISO9001, sells its products directly to the retail customer through its own website and also through a network of independent stores. Prices for the products are identical irrespective of where they are purchased from. Prices on the website are updated from an Excel spreadsheet and dealer price lists are communicated through a different Excel spreadsheet. The two spreadsheets are maintained by two different people.

The existing, and potential, waste here is the fact that the two charts could be replaced with one, and with the dispensation of one the risk of a wrong transposition can be avoided.

None of this, as they say, is rocket science, so why do so many companies fail to recognise the amount of waste generated in the way they process work? The first, in our opinion, is the fact that the detail is left with the jobholder.

Industrial engineering used to be the tour de force within manufacturing. Typically a man would observe another performing an activity and time how long it took to complete that task. There would then ensue an argument over how long the task should really take, and eventually a time somewhere between what the industrial engineer calculated it should be (the shorter time) and the time the operator actually took (the longer time). Let us say that the actual time taken was 80 seconds and the calculated time was 60 seconds, the agreed time was probably 70 seconds. You may well argue that this still represents a waste of 10 seconds. We argue differently. What we have always found interesting is that having demonstrated one time and argued against a shorter time, if one returned to watch that process in operation, with the same operator, a few days later then the time taken was often 55 seconds. What was misunderstood here, and took many years to break the barriers, was that there were two interests at stake: the efficiency of the business and the ability of the operator to maintain a sustained high rate of work that there was little reward for. By working at a pace which beat the agreed time, the operators could earn accumulated periods of relief that were under their control. We are verging into psychological territory here, but the point is that there was still waste in the system and the system itself was wasteful.

The second reason is that companies feel over-regulated in the modern world with the need for audit trails, traceability and compliance. But does this really prevent us all looking for improvements to the business as an everyday issue? What is commonplace as new regulations come into force is that, instinctively, additions are made to existing procedures to accommodate the new regulations, which means more work but no more return. This is, in itself, a waste. It makes the process more cumbersome and the only incentive for doing it is to comply with another piece of legislation. Would it not be a better frame of mind to look for opportunities to remap the process to include the new regulation and make an improvement rather than a burden? Less waste and the same return.

So, once you have reviewed and, in your opinion, removed all of the waste from your process then you should be the best – or are you? Have you considered how your competitors perform, or indeed how someone, perhaps in a different industry, carries out that particular process? If you haven't then benchmarking is what you need.

Chapter 26

Benchmarking

You now have your business under control: you know your processes, your cash flow and cash management are all positive, people are making the maximum contribution and you are measuring what you do to understand patterns and trends and to take appropriate timely action. What else can you do? Be the best.

Being the best is not purely about beating your competition. It is about being as good as you possibly can be. To know that, you need to compare your performance with others that are good at what they do. They do not have to be in the same industry, but they may have a process need identical to yours and which they perform better. Compare, learn from them and get better yourself.

We know of many companies that have undertaken an exercise of this type because they were in trouble and could not ignore the fact that there were plenty of areas in their business that needed improvement. As a general example, look at the Western car industry in the late 1970s into the 80s. They were astonished at how quickly the Japanese were taking volume worldwide from them by producing cars with better reliability at cheaper prices. There was an exodus of auto executives to Japan to learn their secrets only to find that the Japanese had been taught by an American who was ignored in his own country. After the Second World War, Japan was on its knees and the devastation was obvious to anyone who looked out of any window. The result was Just in time, Kaizen, Kanban and a host of other processes that continually had businesses being efficient in stock control, quality management and other essential elements of the business. But they also learned from one another. They found out who did things the best and not only copied them, but improved upon the best when they implemented the practices into their own businesses.

This last point is important. When a Japanese auto executive was asked whether he was concerned about competitors examining how he did things so that the interrogating company could make those improvements to their own businesses, his answer was relaxed. By the time they take away what they have seen and implemented it, he said, Japan would have improved on it and still be ahead.

However, new entrants to the market were not so naïve. Proton worked very closely with Mitsubishi Motors Corporation and Mitsubishi allowed free access to Proton. Proton did not merely copy the systems they witnessed in Japan, they understood them in detail and improved upon them back in Malaysia, causing Mitsubishi a few headaches in the process.

Benchmarking allows us to see how good we really are and how much scope there is for more improvement – continuously. Find out how others do what you do, at the process level, and then analyse and improve. That will give you a short-term advantage until they catch up by which time you will have improved again.

Surely, this is what we should all be aiming to achieve in our businesses – learning from others but using our own skills and talents to improve on what is already better. There is every reason to leapfrog the competition and not just keep up, and every reason to lead and not to follow.

Chapter 27

The Value of Advice

Experience, as the saying goes, is what you get half a second after you really needed it. Advice, on the other hand, is available well ahead of the event and should be obtained from someone who gained the experience in the past for one to apply it in an appropriate way to the exact situation.

In business this is important to a company fulfilling its potential and it is a source of support that the majority of business owners do not consider until after it is needed. A recent survey of business owners showed that 65% of respondents had not sought any professional business advice (including accountant and lawyer) in the previous three years. This is a response from business owners still in business. So what of those who are no longer in business?

The statistics are quite staggering. Fifty per cent of new start-up companies will not be around by the end of year one, and only 10% will still be in existence at the end of year five. This begs the question as to why there is such a rate of attrition when every one of those start-ups was born from a business idea that was, at least, going to generate enough income to provide a living for the business owner. How many from the 50% of businesses that didn't see their second trading year, did not seek any professional advice?

We think that business owners are like car owners, and there are three types:

1. The owner who reads the owner's manual and religiously follows the service routines no matter what – even if the car is running perfectly well.
2. The owner who doesn't follow the service routine but has an acute sense of when things are not running well and then puts the car with a qualified technician to assess the problem and provide a fix and suggestions on how to avoid the problem in the future.
3. The owner who does not follow the servicing routines and even when an unusual sound is heard it is ignored while the car is still running. Eventually the car will break down some miles from home and friends and on a motorway. The owner is not a member of a costly recovery service and is left astonished at both the lack of options and the price being demanded for the tow truck to even just move the car off the motorway to a repair centre.

What kind of car owner are you?

Our advice is, keep your car in the best running condition that you can – which will mean using a specialist. Don't get a tyre fitter to retune your engine, or a gearbox engineer to change your exhaust. Use a garage that you can trust who always does a good job and refers you to other specialists when the occasion requires. Use the right specialist and you will get the best results. Even if your car is running well, you will get a better performance, petrol consumption with overall cost and time efficiency by following the right advice and adapting the way you drive.

Chapter 28

Coaching is Not a Weakness

After the previous section it is probably necessary to distinguish between advice and coaching. They should not be confused and there are many service companies around who are very good advisors but are not coaches. That is, they will point the way but they will not increase your ability and efficiency in getting there. The most potent example of coaching in recent years, I believe, is the Team GB cycling team. It also demonstrates the difference between advising and coaching.

British cycling has had many advisors over the decades in attempts to improve the performance of our national riders in international competitions and through that we have seen only limited individual pinnacles: Tommy Simpson, Barry Hogan. Advice has been about the 'what' and very little about working with the individual to get them to perform to his or her fullest potential. The two go hand in glove but whoever told the team to make their wheels round only made the bike quicker and not the rider quicker, fitter and cannier. What has been achieved in Team GB is a combination of the physical 'what' with the psychological and physiological 'how' in a number of elements and added them together to determine a world beating performance over a period of time.

In business it is similar. As a business owner you hopefully have the talent and you hopefully have the tools you need to do the job. However, as an individual you may not have the full scope of skills, experience, technique or knowledge to perform as best as you possibly can to grow every element of a fast growth business in the making. Examine how tennis players, or golfers, improve their ranking following the engagement of a new coach. Andy Murray didn't get a new injection of talent when he appointed Ivan Lendl, but he did get a new edge to his game that saw his competitiveness at the court of the top four improve. He has now changed coach again, which demonstrates recognition of what is required for the next stage in his development.

And another thing, coaching isn't necessarily all about a single point of contact. Unless you are a one-man band, companies work most effectively as teams and it could be the team that needs coaching and not just the owner. Going back to a sporting analogy, there are many distinguished team coaches who have transformed the performance of a set of players and developed a better team – just look at what Clive Woodward did with the England Rugby Union side.

But enough of the sports analogies – let's get back to business. Richard Branson had Freddie Laker, and Steve Jobs had Bill Campbell. A coach will not take anything away from you or constrain you. Rather a coach will be able to give you the small incremental improvements in a number of areas and it is when you aggregate all of these improvements that you will witness the significant overall improvement in your business performance.

Confucius said, 'The mechanic that would perfect his work must first sharpen his tools.' Coaching not only sharpens the tools in your toolbox, but it will extend the number of tools that you have available, improve your skill in using the right tool at the most appropriate time, and generally ensure that you use the tools in the most effective way with a resulting:

- better revenue,
- improved profits,
- better cost and time efficiency, and
- most probably, give you a better life-work balance.

Final Thoughts

Thank you for taking the time to read our book. We really hope that you have gained useful reminders and new knowledge from your time and effort. We have met very few business owners who have a degree in how to start, grow, establish and successfully exit a business. It is thus OK for you to not ever know everything. You can, however, surround yourself with the right people and tools that can give you all the knowledge you need to achieve your objectives. We are also keen for you to make this book work for your individual business and to help you on your way we are offering a special additional feature to the Advantage Business Partnerships Strategic Performance Assessment (SPA) (valued at over £199.00 plus VAT).

Go to www.advantagebusinessltd.com and complete the SPA questionnaire using the code SBO. Once you have submitted your answers you will receive a personal debrief from either Daryl or Garry.

Be successful.